Bon Appetit!

50 Soup Recipes

Barbara O'neill

Introduction

Hot soups began to be prepared with the invention of the first primitive utensils. Now fish, meat, chicken and vegetable soups are impressively diverse.

Soups are also good because you can prepare a full saucepan for several days, even for a large family. For people who do not eat meat, there are soups with seafood, mushrooms, lentils and other legumes. Of course, I also have classic recipes: borscht, chicken broth, pea soup, cabbage soup. To suit all taste!

Chicken & Chickpeas Tomato Soup

I suggest varying the usual soups with peas and beans with other legumes.
For example, this recipe for soup with chicken, tomatoes and chickpeas.
If you do not want to spend time soaking and boiling chickpeas,
take canned chickpeas.

Ingredients

Chicken fillet - 1
Chickpeas - 1 can
Tomato paste - 1-2 tablespoons
Carrots - 2
Bell pepper - 1
Onions - 1
Tomatoes - 2
Chili - 2
Garlic - 2 cloves
Spices and seasonings - 2 teaspoons

Instructions

1. Boil the chicken fillets in boiling water for about 30 minutes, remove and chop.
2. Add the chopped carrots, onions and peppers to the broth.
3. Peel the tomatoes and chop them.
4. After 5-7 minutes, add the tomatoes, tomato paste, chickpeas and chicken to the soup.
5. Boil for 5 minutes, season and add the chopped chili and garlic.
6. Stir well and remove the soup from the heat.

Rice, Potato & Chicken Kharcho

This traditional Georgian dish will be to the liking of everyone who tries it.
Boiled, classic kharcho of chicken with rice and potatoes, aroma and
spicy taste of spices and herbs. Any dinner will be perfect
if there is kharcho soup on the table.

Ingredients

Chicken – 18 oz
Rice - 4 tablespoons
Potatoes - 4
Onions - 2
Tomatoes - 4
Water - 3 liters
Garlic - 3 cloves
Olive oil - 2 tablespoons
Cilantro - 1 bunch
Bay leaf - 2
Khmeli-Suneli - to taste
Peppercorns - to taste
Salt - to taste

Instructions

1. Wash the meat, cut it into small pieces.
2. Peel the potatoes and cut them into cubes. Peel the onion and garlic and chop finely. Wash and cube the tomatoes.
3. Boil the meat, when it is cooked, remove the broth from the heat. Take out the meat and put the broth to boil again. Add potatoes and rice to the broth.
4. Chop the meat and add it to the potatoes and rice.
5. Pour vegetable oil into a frying pan. Fry the onion and garlic until golden. Add the tomatoes and stir well. Stew until half cooked and remove from the heat.
6. Add spices to the soup, salt, add the dressing and cook for 15 minutes. Finely chop the cilantro. When serving, sprinkle the soup with cilantro.

Mashed Potato Soup with Leek

Mashed potato soup turns out much tastier and more interesting than it seems at first glance. Especially if you add spices and leek. When I want something more spicy, I add chili.

Ingredients

Potatoes – 25 oz
Carrots - 1
Leeks - 2
Butter - 2 tablespoons
Spices and seasonings - 1 teaspoon
Cream (20%) - 200 ml
Chili pepper - 1 pinch

Instructions

1. Boil the potatoes, drain, but do not pour out the potato water.
2. Grate the carrots, finely chop the leeks and fry in butter.
3. Fill with cream, bring to the boil and send the roast to the potatoes.
4. Mash with a blender, bring the potato broth to the desired consistency and season.

Tomato & Bean Soup

Doesn't your family like soups? Try making them in a new way –
for example, use this recipe for tomato bean soup. My family loves
this soup. It's cooked with vegetables.

Ingredients

Beans (dry) - 1 cup
Tomatoes - 3
Bell pepper - 1
Celery (stalks) – ½ cup
Carrots - 1
Onion - 1
Olive oil - 2 tablespoons
Oregano – ½ teaspoon
Salt - to taste
Water - 2.5 liters

Instructions

1. Wash the beans and soak them in cold water for 2 hours.
2. Put the beans in a saucepan, pour in clean water and boil for 40 minutes over medium heat.
3. Slice the carrots, celery, peeled onion and bell pepper.
4. Remove the peel from the tomatoes. Chop the tomatoes in a blender.
5. In a heated pan with oil, fry the onion and carrots until golden.
6. Pour in the bell pepper and continue cooking for 7 minutes.
7. In a saucepan with beans, add celery, tomato puree and roast. Boil for 15 minutes.
8. Season with salt and oregano, turn off and leave under the lid for 20 minutes.

Salmon, Cod & Pearl Soup

Many people add various cereals to the fish soup to make the soup thicker and more nourishing. Today I suggest trying an interesting recipe with pearl. We will cook it with salmon and cod fillets.
An amazing dish with a fabulous flavor!

Ingredients

Salmon (fillet) – 15 oz
Cod (fillet) – 15 oz
Chickpeas – ½ cup
Potatoes – 10 oz
Carrots - 1
Onion - 1
Vegetable oil - 2 tablespoons
Bay leaf - 2 pieces
Lemon zest - 0.5 teaspoon
Salt - to taste
Water (filtered) - 2 liters
Dill (for serving) - 2 sprigs

Instructions

1. Wash the pearl and soak in water for half an hour.
2. Wash salmon and cod fillets, cut into small pieces.
3. Peel the potatoes and onions, chop them. Grate the carrots.
4. Put the cod and bay leaves in a pot, pour cold water and cook for 20 minutes.
5. Remove the cod with a skimmer and set aside.
6. Add the salmon, the pearls and potatoes to the pot. Cook for half an hour over low heat.
7. Fry the onions and carrots in vegetable oil until golden.
8. Add the fried vegetables, cod and lemon zest to the saucepan with the soup. Continue cooking for 5 minutes. Salt, turn off and leave under the lid for 10 minutes. Add chopped dill when serving.

Green Borscht with Sorrel

Green borscht with sorrel is a classic of Ukrainian cuisine.
Today I will tell you how to cook it. I prefer to serve it with a poached egg,
but you can boil the egg to your taste.

Ingredients

Chicken – 10 oz
Sorrel – ½ cup
Potatoes - 3
Onion - 1
Greens - 1 cup
Egg whites - 1
Spices and seasonings - 1 tablespoon
Celery – 2

Instructions

1. Boil the chicken until cooked through. Add the sliced potatoes and cook for 15 minutes.
2. Chop the onion and celery and fry for about 5 minutes. Add to the soup.
3. Chop the sorrel and greens, add them to the soup and bring to a boil. Season.
4. Pour in the egg white, stirring. Boil the green borscht for 1 minute or 2 and remove from the heat.

Chicken Pea Soup

Today I want to share with you the easiest pea soup with chicken broth.
The main thing is that peas and other legumes are a useful and necessary food.

Ingredients

Chicken – 10 oz
Peas - 1 cup
Carrots - 2
Onion - 1
Garlic - 2 cloves
Turmeric powder - 1 teaspoon
Spices and seasonings - 1 teaspoon

Instructions

1. Boil the chicken until cooked through, chop and set aside.
2. Rinse the peas and cook in the boiling broth for 20-25 minutes.
3. Add the chopped carrots and onions, add the chicken and the spices and garlic.
4. Cook for 15 minutes.

Meat Soup with Beef Tongue

Let's try to cook soup with beef tongue. The soup will be very tasty.
Serve the dish for dinner and enjoy it.

Ingredients

Beef tongue (boiled) – 10 oz
Beef (boiled) – 1 cup
Carrots - 1
Onion - 1
Tomato paste - 3 tablespoons
Vegetable oil - 3 tablespoons
Sweet pepper - to taste
Ground black pepper - to taste
Salt - to taste
Meat broth - 2.5 liters

Instructions

1. Clean the cow's tongue and cut into small cubes.
2. Chop the beef, sausages, cucumbers, carrots and onions.
3. In a heated pan with oil, fry the onion and carrots until golden.
4. Add the beef, tomato paste, 200 ml of broth and the ground black pepper. Simmer for 5 minutes.
5. Add beef tongue and roast and simmer for 10 minutes. Season with salt. Season with salt. Leave the soup under the lid for 15 minutes.

Tasty Pea Soup

Pea soup is a hearty, delicious and easy-to-make dish. For example, this recipe with vegetables, smoked meats and spices!

Ingredients

Smoked meat (to taste) – 12 oz
Peas - 1 cup
Potatoes – 10 oz
Carrots - 2
Onions - 2
Salt - 1 teaspoon
Peppercorns - 1 teaspoon
Spices and seasonings - 1 teaspoon
Garlic - 4 cloves

Instructions

1. Soak the peas overnight. Wash, pour in the water and boil for an hour.
2. Chop the smoked meat and vegetables. Add to the peas and simmer for 20 minutes.
3. Add the garlic and spices, simmer for 5-7 minutes, and remove the soup from the heat.

Tomato Mashed Potato Soup with Basil

This mashed potato soup is so quick and easy to prepare
that everyone will make it.

Ingredients

Tomatoes (in tomato juice) – 25 oz
Water - 500 ml
Cream - 200 ml
Italian seasoning - 2 teaspoons
Spices (to taste) - 1 teaspoon
Garlic - 6 cloves
Basil – 1 cup
Salt - to taste
Onion – 1

Instructions

1. Finely chop the onion and garlic and fry until golden.
2. Chop the tomatoes in a blender and add to the onion.
3. Add the water, bring the soup to a boil and add the spices.
4. Cook for 15 minutes on low heat.
5. Add the cream and the chopped basil.
6. Boil for 3 minutes and remove the soup from the heat.

Cauliflower Cream Soup with Broccoli & Feta

I suggest adding to your cooking records with this recipe - cream soup with cauliflower, broccoli and feta. Delicious combination of flavors, creamy texture and delicious aroma!

Ingredients

Cauliflower – 15 oz
Broccoli – 10 oz
Onion - 1
Cream (33%) - 5 tablespoons
Vegetable oil - 2 tablespoons
Ground black pepper - to taste
Salt - to taste
Feta (for serving) – ½ cup
Parsley (to serve) - 2 sprigs
Chicken broth - 1.5 liters

Instructions

1. Cut the cauliflower and broccoli into small florets.
2. Peel the onion and chop finely.
3. Boil the broth, add the broccoli and cauliflower and simmer for 7 minutes.
4. Add the oil to a frying pan, add the onion and fry until golden.
5. Pour the fried onion into the saucepan with the vegetables and simmer for 7 minutes.
6. Remove the soup from the heat and puree with a blender.
7. Add the cream, salt and ground black pepper. Warm over low heat for 3-4 minutes, but do not boil.
8. When serving, add crumbled feta to the plate.

Pea & Lentil Soup

All legumes can be mixed together in different dishes. Remember,
split peas take a little longer to cook than lentils. I'll be happy to explain these
details in this recipe.

Ingredients

Peas (split) – ½ cup
Red lentils – ½ cup
Smoked meat – 10 oz
Onions - 2
Carrots - 2
Turmeric - 1 teaspoon
Paprika - 1 teaspoon
Peppercorns – ½ teaspoon
Salt - 1 teaspoon
Herbs – ½ cup

Instructions

1. Fill the peas with water and simmer for 10 minutes.
2. Add the lentils and simmer for 10 minutes. Put the chopped smoked meat into the soup.
3. Chop the onion, grate the carrots and fry until soft. Also add to the soup.
4. Cook until the ingredients are ready. Add herbs and spices, and after 2 minutes remove the pea soup from the fire.

Meat Broth with Noodle

Noodle is a very tasty product. The main thing is broth, more noodles and any additives. I suggest making a basic recipe!

Ingredients

Water - 2.5 liters
Meat (on the bone) – 17 oz
Carrots - 1
Onion - 1
Egg noodles – 1 cup
Turmeric - 1 teaspoon
Butter – 2 tablespoons
Herbs - 2 sprigs
Ground black pepper - 1 pinch
Salt - 1 teaspoon

Instructions

1. Fill the meat and peeled carrots with cold water and simmer over low heat without a lid for about 1.5 hours, skimming off the foam. Take out the meat and carrots.
2. Finely chop the onion and fry it in butter until golden brown. Add turmeric and stir.
3. Bring the broth to a boil, add the onions and noodles, and simmer for 4-5 minutes. At the end, add salt and black pepper.
4. Garnish the broth with chopped herbs and carrot slices.

Seafood Soup

Have a little feast! Call your friends, get some beautiful dishes and make a delicious seafood soup. Everyone will love this original soup. Serve with garlic crackers, lemon or lime.

Ingredients

Seafood (to taste) – 17 oz
Onion - 1
Garlic - 3 cloves
Olive oil - 2 tablespoons
Tomato juice - 150 ml
Lemon juice - 1 tablespoon
Black pepper - 3 peas
Parsley - 2 sprigs
Salt - to taste
Fish broth - 2.5 liters

Instructions

1. Peel the onion and garlic.
2. Heat oil in a frying pan, add onion and garlic and fry until golden.
3. Add the seafood and fry for 7-10 minutes.
4. Add the tomato and lemon juice and simmer under a lid for 5 minutes.
5. In a saucepan, boil the broth, add the roast, black pepper, peas and simmer for 10 minutes after boiling.
6. Season with salt, sprinkle with chopped parsley and remove from the heat.

Mashed Potato Soup with Bacon & Cheese

Mashed potato soup is a simple soup. For example, this bacon and cheese soup is very hearty, flavorful and savory.

Ingredients

Potatoes – 15 oz
Vegetable broth - 700 ml
Cream - 200 ml
Onion - 1
Olive oil - 1 tablespoon
Spices and seasonings - 1 teaspoon
Cheddar cheese – ½ cup
Bacon – ½ cup
Herbs - 4 sprigs

Instructions

1. Slice the potatoes and boil in the broth.
2. Fry the onion in oil until golden, add it to the potatoes and blend.
3. Add the cream, warm the soup once again and season.
4. Fry finely chopped bacon in a frying pan, without oil.
5. Top the soup with the bacon, grated cheddar and chopped herbs.

Mushroom Soup

The flavor of wild mushroom soup is impossible to resist after the first breath!
I will tell you how to prepare the ingredients and how long to boil them.

Ingredients

Water - 2 liters
Wild mushrooms – 20 oz
Onions - 1
Carrot - 1
Salt – ½ teaspoon
Ground black pepper - 1 pinch
Vegetable oil - 1 tablespoon
Butter - 2 tablespoons

Instructions

1. Clean the mushrooms, rinse well and slice.
2. Boil them for 30 minutes in salted water, drain in a colander.
3. Bring 2 liters of clean water to a boil, send the mushrooms in and simmer for 30 minutes.
4. Finely chop the onions and carrots and fry until golden.
5. Send the roast into the soup and boil for 5-7 minutes. Add the spices to taste.

Pea Soup with Vegetables & Minced Meat

Pea soup is prepared not only with smoked meat or whole pieces of meat, but also with minced meat. In addition, I suggest adding more vegetables. For this recipe, I recommend using green peas, fresh or frozen.

Ingredients

Pork – 1 cup
Beef – 1 cup
Peas (green) – 1 cup
String beans – ½ cup
Corn – ½ cup
Tomatoes - 2
Bell pepper - 1
Potatoes - 3
Carrots - 1
Onion - 1
Spices and seasonings - 2 teaspoons
Olive oil - 2 tablespoons

Instructions

1. Grind the pork and beef through a meat grinder.
2. Fry the mince in a frying pan with oil.
3. Finely chop all the vegetables and add to the mince. First carrots, onions and peppers, and after 3-4 minutes all other products.
4. Simmer for 3 minutes and pour in water or broth.
5. Season and simmer the soup until the ingredients are cooked.

Ukrainian Borscht

To make the color of Ukrainian borscht brighter, and the taste richer - add a little tomato paste to it. In the recipe, I will tell you in detail how and when to do it.

Ingredients

Chicken fillet - 1
Beet - 1
Tomato paste - 3 tablespoons
Cabbage – 1 cup
Carrots - 1
Bell pepper - 1
Onion - 1
Spices and seasonings - 1 tablespoon
Potatoes – 1 cup

Instructions

1. Boil the chicken until cooked through. Add the sliced potatoes and cook for 10 minutes.
2. Grate the carrots and beet. Chop the onion and pepper. Fry everything together for about 7 minutes over medium heat, stirring.
3. Add cabbage and tomato paste to the vegetables. Pour in a little broth, simmer for 7 minutes and season.
4. Send the roast to the saucepan, boil the borscht for 5 minutes and remove from the heat.

Quail Soup with Halushky

What could be more delicious than quail soup? And if you add halushky to it, it will also be hearty. Making this soup for lunch is very easy. The main thing is to observe one important rule - do not overcook quail. Tender meat will be enough for 25-30 minutes.

Ingredients

For soup:
Quail - 2
Potatoes -1 cup
Carrots - 1
Onion - 1
Herbs (various) - 4 sprigs
Vegetable oil - 3 tablespoons
Salt - to taste
Water - 3 liters
For halushky:
Chicken eggs - 1
Flour - 5 tablespoons
Ground black pepper - to taste
Salt – ½ teaspoon

Instructions

1. Peel the potatoes and onions and chop. Grate the carrots with a fine grater.
2. Clean the quails, cover with cold water and simmer for 30 minutes.
3. Remove the quails to a plate and cool slightly. Separate the meat from the bones and chop.
4. Heat the oil in a frying pan, add the onion and carrots and fry until golden.
5. In a saucepan, add the potatoes, roast, chopped quail meat and cook for 5 minutes.
6. In a bowl, mix the flour, egg, salt and ground black pepper.
7. Pour in 120 ml of the hot soup from the saucepan and knead the dough.
8. Using a dessert spoon, scoop the dough and drop it into the boiling soup. Cook the soup for 7 minutes.
9. Add salt, finely chopped herbs and turn off after 2 minutes.

Pea Puree Soup with Broccoli

Puree soups are good because they allow you to combine the most unusual and unexpected ingredients. For example, today I propose to make this pea puree soup with broccoli. I am sure you have not tasted such an original recipe yet.

Ingredients

Vegetable broth - 1.5 liters
Peas - 2 cups
Broccoli - 1
Leeks - 1
Olive oil - 1 tablespoon
Spices and seasonings - 1 teaspoon
Thyme - 2 sprigs

Instructions

1. Soak the peas in advance and then boil in the vegetable broth until tender.
2. Add the cauliflower and simmer for 5 minutes.
3. Fry the chopped leeks and add to the soup. Cook for 5 minutes.
4. Whisk with a blender, add the spices and thyme, and serve.

Vegetable Soup with Pasta

If you think that vegetable vegetarian soups are always very light –
you just haven't seen this recipe with pasta and beans yet.
The soup turns out very thick, hearty and very tasty - the perfect
choice for any time of year.

Ingredients

Vegetable broth - 2.5 liters
Potatoes - 2
Pasta - 1 cup
Carrots - 1
Celery - 1
Zucchini - 1
Beans (canned) – ½ cup
String beans – 1 cup
Green peas – 1 cup
Spices and seasonings - 2 teaspoons

Instructions

1. Boil the vegetable broth and add the potatoes, carrots and celery.
2. After 5-7 minutes, add all the vegetables, pasta and beans.
3. Season the soup and simmer until the pasta is cooked.

Pork & Chickpeas Soup

Soup with pork and chickpeas turns out nutritious and very hearty. This soup is perfect for the cold season. There is nothing complicated in the recipe, but the chickpeas will need to be soaked in advance.

Ingredients

Pork – 15 oz
Chickpeas - 1 cup
Potatoes - 3
Carrots - 1
Onion - 1
Vegetable oil - 30 ml
Black pepper - 3 peas
Laurel leaf - 2
Salt - to taste
Water - 2.5 liters

Instructions

1. Rinse the chickpeas and leave to soak for 5 hours.
2. Cut the pork into small pieces and place in a saucepan.
3. Add the chickpeas, bay leaf, black pepper and cold water. Cook for 50 minutes over low heat.
4. Peel and chop the potatoes, carrot and onion.
5. Heat oil in a frying pan, add the onion and carrot and fry until golden.
6. Add the potatoes and roast to the saucepan. Boil for 15 minutes. Add salt.

Chicken Soup with Beans & Spinach

This chicken soup catches the eye with its rich color. It will be liked by lovers of spinach and greens. And canned beans make it very hearty and nutritious.

Ingredients

Chicken fillet - 1
Beans (canned) – 1 cup
Spinach - 1 bunch
Herbs - 1 bunch
Green onions - 1 bunch
Garlic - 2 cloves
Spices and seasonings - 1 teaspoon
Water – 2 liters

Instructions

1. Boil the chicken for about 35 minutes, remove and cut into cubes.
2. Finely chop the spinach, spring onion and herbs. Chop the garlic.
3. Lightly simmer in a pan.
4. Send the greens, beans and chicken into the boiling broth, season to taste and boil for 5-7 minutes.

Pea Puree Soup with Lentil

Pea combines perfectly in soups with other legumes. For example, with lentils in this flavorful, hearty and brightly colored puree soup. Sprinkle it with smoked paprika, and serve with crispy breadcrumbs.

Ingredients

Peas – 1 cup
Lentils – 1 cup
Carrots - 2
Onion - 1
Bell pepper - 1
Spices and seasonings - 1 teaspoon

Instructions

1. Boil the peas and lentils in water.
2. Finely chop the onions and pepper, grate the carrots and fry the vegetables until soft.
3. Mix everything together, whisk with a blender and season to taste.

Pea Soup with Smoked Chicken

Smoked meat is the perfect base for pea soup. And they can be any kind. It is not only hunting sausages or pork ribs. Today I propose to prepare your favorite soup with fragrant smoked chicken!

Ingredients

Pea – 15 oz
Meat broth - 2 liters
Potatoes - 4
Herbs – ½ cup
Smoked chicken (fillet) - 1
Carrots - 1
Onion – 1

Instructions

1. Soak and wash the peas in advance. Boil in the broth until tender.
2. Add chopped smoked chicken and potatoes, 20 minutes before the end of cooking.
3. Chop the onion and the carrot, lightly fry, and add to the soup.
4. Cook until the potatoes are ready, add chopped herbs, season to taste and simmer the soup for 5 minutes.

Vegetarian Kharcho

Kharcho is a traditional Georgian soup with beef. Few people know that the vegetarian version of this dish is not only lighter, but tasty too.

Ingredients

Potatoes – 15 oz
Rice – ½ cup
Onions - 1
Carrots - 2
Garlic (clove) - 4
Tomato paste - 3 tablespoons
Sunflower oil - 4 tablespoons
Khmeli-suneli – ½ teaspoon
Bay leaf – 2

Instructions

1. Put water on the fire. Add diced potatoes, washed rice, salt and simmer for 10-15 minutes. Grate the carrots.
2. Heat a frying pan with vegetable oil. Put the chopped garlic and onion on it. Fry for 3-5 minutes. Add tomato paste, khmeli-suneli, pepper and carrots. Stew for 5 minutes over low heat.
3. Pour the contents of the pan into a saucepan, add the bay leaves and herbs. Boil for a few minutes.

Vegan Pea & Vegetable Soup

Specially for you, a recipe for pea soup with vegetables. The soup is rich, flavorful and very tasty.

Ingredients

Pea (dry) - 1 cup
Green peas – ½ cup
Potatoes - 3
Carrots - 1
Onion - 1
Garlic - 2 cloves
Vegetable oil - 2 tablespoons
Salt - to taste
Parsley - 5 sprigs
Water (filtered) - 2 liters

Instructions

1. Wash the dry peas, soak in cold water for 5-6 hours.
2. Wash the pea again and put into a saucepan of boiling water and cook for 45 minutes on low heat.
3. Chop the green beans, carrots, peeled potatoes and onions.
4. Heat the oil in a pan, add the onion and carrot and fry for 5-7 minutes.
5. In a saucepan with peas, add the potatoes, string beans and roast. Cook for 10 minutes.
6. Add green peas, press garlic, salt and turn off.

Sausage & Green Pea Soup

If you haven't tried making sausage soup yet, I recommend it! Of course, it's not as healthy as a fresh piece of meat, but it's very fast.
Add more vegetables and green pea.

Ingredients

Sausages - 4-6
Potatoes - 3
Carrots - 2
Green peas – 1 cup
String beans – ½ cup
Herbs – ½ cup
Spices and seasonings - 1 teaspoon
Salt - to taste

Instructions

1. Cut the potatoes into cubes and the sausages and carrots into circles.
2. Boil water, put potatoes and carrots in it and cook for 15 minutes.
3. Add the sausages, peas and string beans and simmer for 10 minutes.
4. Season the soup to taste and add herbs.

Pea & Cabbage Soup

Cabbage is very rarely used in pea soup. I'm sharing a delicious everyday recipe that everyone will love. It's easy to prepare!

Ingredients

Chicken – 10 oz
Pea – 1 cup
Potatoes - 3
Cabbage – 1 cup
Onion - 1
Carrot - 1
Spices and seasonings - 1 teaspoon

Instructions

1. Boil the chicken. Add peas to the broth and simmer for 20 minutes.
2. Add the potatoes, and after 5-7 minutes, add the cabbage. Take the chicken out, shred the meat and return to the saucepan.
3. During this time, fry the onions and carrots and put into the soup.
4. Cook until the vegetables are ready. At the end, season the soup.

Zucchini Cream Soup with Spinach

It is enough to add a little cream to the zucchini - and here the cream-soup becomes even more tender and pleasant. And for a more intense flavor, I use spinach and spices. The dish turns out very light and low-calorie, but very tasty.

Ingredients

Zucchini - 2
Cream - 200 ml
Vegetable broth – 1 liter
Spinach – ½ cup
Garlic - 3 cloves
Sea salt - 1 teaspoon
Peppercorns (ground) - 1 teaspoon
Herbs - 1 teaspoon
Butter - 2 tablespoons
Olive oil - 2 tablespoons

Instructions

1. Finely chop the spinach and fry for a couple of minutes in oil and butter.
2. Add the crushed garlic and diced zucchini. Fry for 5 minutes.
3. Add vegetable broth and simmer for 5 minutes and blend. Add cream, add all the spices and stir.

Cheese & Broccoli Soup

For this recipe, I use two kinds of cheese at once - cream and cheddar.
In addition, you will need broccoli and other vegetables.
And I recommend serving it with slices of toasted baguette.

Ingredients

Chicken broth - 2 liters
Broccoli - 1
Carrots - 2
Potatoes - 2
Leeks - 1
Cream cheese – ½ cup
Cheddar cheese – ½ cup
Spices and seasonings - 2 teaspoons

Instructions

1. Finely chop the potatoes, carrots and onions. Add to the boiling broth.
2. Chop the broccoli into florets and add to the broth. Cook for about 5 minutes.
3. Add spices and cream cheese. Continue to simmer until it melts.
4. Remove the soup from the heat and sprinkle with grated cheddar.

Asparagus Puree Soup

This puree soup is slightly like something between onion and bean soup. It's easier to try it once than to explain it in words.

Ingredients

Potatoes – 10 oz
Asparagus – 25 oz
Shallots - 1
Chicken broth - 800 ml
Wine (white dry) - 150 ml
Cream (20%) - 150 ml
Spices and seasonings - 1 teaspoon
Olive oil - 2 tablespoons

Instructions

1. Finely chop the potatoes and asparagus.
2. Boil the water and boil the asparagus tops for 2-3 minutes.
3. Slice the shallot and fry until golden in olive oil.
4. Add the potatoes and asparagus stalks and fry for 7-8 minutes.
5. Pour in the white wine and allow it to evaporate.
6. Add the broth and simmer the soup for 15 minutes after boiling over medium heat.
7. Add the asparagus tops, simmer for 5 minutes and puree the soup with a blender.
8. Add the warm cream and season to taste.

Broccoli & Herbs Soup Puree

Cream or puree soup can be made with almost any ingredients.
For example, today I want to share one of my favorite recipes with
broccoli and herbs.

Ingredients

Broccoli - 1
Vegetable broth - 1 liter
Parsley – ½ cup
Dill – ½ cup
Basil – ½ cup
Garlic - 5 cloves
Spices and seasonings - 2 teaspoons
Cream - 150 ml

Instructions

1. Cut the broccoli into florets, place in the boiling vegetable stock and simmer until soft.
2. Finely chop the herbs and garlic with a knife.
3. Chop the broccoli with a blender, add the cream and mix.
4. Season, add the herbs and garlic, mix again with a blender and bring to a boil. Remove the soup from the heat.

Tomato Soup with Cream Cheese

An interesting variation of tomato cream soup - this time with soft cream cheese. And the flavor becomes softer and more harmonious - even children will like it.

Ingredients

Tomatoes – 35 oz
Onions - 1
Garlic - 3 cloves
Cream cheese – 1 cup
Tomato paste - 1-2 tablespoons
Butter – 2 tablespoons
Sugar - 1 pinch
Salt - 1 pinch
Spices and seasonings - 1 teaspoon

Instructions

1. Peel the tomatoes and chop all the vegetables.
2. Lightly fry the onion and garlic in butter, pour a glass of water and bring to a boil.
3. Add the tomatoes and simmer for 15 minutes over medium heat.
4. Add the tomato paste and all the spices, and after 5 minutes, remove the pot from the heat.
5. Whisk the soup with a blender, add the cream cheese and blend thoroughly.

Chicken Cream Soup

Chicken combines best with cream, and this chicken soup is clear proof of that. I'm telling you, how to cook it.

Ingredients

Chicken fillet - 1
Water - 1.5 liters
Cream - 400 ml
Butter – 2 tablespoons
Flour - 1-2 tablespoons
Nutmeg – ½ teaspoon
Ground black pepper – ½ teaspoon
Salt - 1 teaspoon
Carrots - 1
Leek - 1
Parsley - 4 sprigs

Instructions

1. Cut up the chicken, add water and boil until tender.
2. Add sliced carrots and chopped leeks to the boiling broth.
3. Fry the flour in butter until golden, add the cream and mix well.
4. Add all the spices and carefully pour the sauce into the chicken soup.
5. Mix well again and simmer for 5 minutes.
6. Add chopped parsley and spices.

Pea Puree Soup with Spinach

Green peas and spinach give bright and rich color to such a puree soup. And the delicate texture and creamy flavor in the soup.

Ingredients

Chicken fillet - 1
Peas (green) – 2 cups
Cream - 100 ml
Spinach – 1 cup
Spices and seasonings - 1 teaspoon
Olive oil - 1 tablespoon

Instructions

1. Boil the chicken fillets until tender. Put the green peas in the same place and boil.
2. Chop spinach and fry lightly in olive oil.
3. Mix the ingredients in a blender with the spices.
4. Pour in the cream and whisk the soup again, cook on the stove for 3 minutes and remove from the heat.

Celery Puree Soup

Celery puree soup is a diet soup. It is very light and quite low-calorie. A pleasant creamy color completes the soup. Decorate it with your favorite herbs and spices!

Ingredients

Celery - 3-4 stalks
Celery root - 1
Potatoes - 2
Onion - 1
Vegetable broth - 500 ml
Spices and seasonings - 1 teaspoon

Instructions

1. Finely chop the onion, stalks and celery root and fry lightly.
2. Pour in the broth, bring to the boil, and add the diced potatoes.
3. Cook the soup until the potatoes are cooked, puree with a blender and season.

Spinach & Broccoli Puree Soup

Spinach and broccoli are the perfect combination for beautiful and delicious puree soups. Bright green color, thick consistency and excellent taste - what else do you need.

Ingredients

Broccoli – 18 oz
Spinach – 10 oz
Cream - 250 ml
Cheese – ½ cup
Onion - 2
Water - 1 liter
Spices and seasonings - 1 teaspoon

Instructions

1. Cut the broccoli into florets and boil for 7 minutes in boiling water.
2. Finely chop the onion and fry until soft. Add the spinach and fry for 2 minutes.
3. Add the roast to the broccoli and simmer for 7 minutes.
4. Grind the soup in a blender, add the cream, grated cheese and spices.
5. Bring the soup back to the boil and simmer until the cheese has dissolved.

Carrot Puree Soup for Children

Carrot puree soup is an invaluable source of vitamins that we need so much in our daily lives. It will be especially useful for children, but adults will surely like it too. I like to serve it with sour cream, or cream cheese.

Ingredients

Carrots – 25 oz
Bell pepper - 1
Cream - 200 ml
Paprika - 1 teaspoon
Spices and seasonings - 1 teaspoon
Garlic - 2 cloves
Butter – 2 tablespoons

Instructions

1. Slice the carrots and bell pepper, and fry in butter and garlic.
2. Fill the vegetables with water and boil until soft.
3. Puree the soup with a blender, add all the spices and cream.
4. Bring back to the boil and remove from the heat.

Pea Puree Soup with Mint

Pea puree soup with mint is one of the most original finds in my selection of recipes. Bean soups are always very hearty, but at the same time, fresh mint leaves add a light and refreshing taste.

Ingredients

Peas (green) – 18 oz
Coconut milk - 200 ml
Vegetable broth - 1 liter
Mint - 4 sprigs
Olive oil - 1 tablespoon
Spices and seasonings - 1 teaspoon

Instructions

1. Bring the broth to the boil, add the green peas and simmer for 10 minutes.
2. Chop everything with a blender. Pour in the coconut milk, add the chopped mint, garlic and spices.
3. Blend again and simmer the soup for 5-7 minutes.

Zucchini & Cheese Soup Puree

For this recipe, I suggest choosing yellow zucchini to make the color more interesting. Any hard cheese will do.

Ingredients

Zucchini - 3
Cheese – ½ cup
Melted cheese – ½ cup
Onion - 2
Garlic - 2 cloves
Breadcrumbs - 4 tablespoons
Vegetable broth - 2 liters
Spices and seasonings - 1 teaspoon

Instructions

1. Chop the onion, garlic and zucchini and fill with water.
2. Bring to a boil and add both grated cheeses and breadcrumbs.
3. Cook the soup until the cheese is melted.
4. Add the spices and puree the soup with a blender.

Leek Soup

Leek soup is a favorite dish. I advise you to try this kind of leek soup. It is a completely different and very tender dish!

Ingredients

Onion - 1
Garlic - 1-2 cloves
Leek - 2 stalks
Potatoes - 3
Butter – 3 tablespoons
Chicken broth - 600 ml
Milk - 200 ml
Salt - 1 teaspoon
Ground black pepper – ½ teaspoon

Instructions

1. Finely chop the vegetables. Fry the onion and garlic until transparent.
2. Add the leeks and potatoes and simmer for a couple of minutes.
3. Pour in the broth and simmer the vegetables for 10 minutes after boiling.
4. Pour in the milk and cream, boil again and simmer for 10 minutes. Season the soup with salt and pepper.
5. Puree the soup with a blender.

Corn Soup Puree

This unusual puree soup is made from canned or frozen corn. However, in summer, you can take whole cobs, boil them in salted water.

Ingredients

Corn – 18 oz
Olive oil - 2 tablespoons
Onion - 1
Carrot - 1
Ground coriander – ½ teaspoon
Ground ginger – ½ teaspoon
Salt - 1 teaspoon
Cream (20%) – ½ cup

Instructions

1. Finely chop the onion and fry in olive oil until soft.
2. Add the carrot and the corn, mix and add the water or the broth. You need about 1.5-2 liters.
3. Add all the spices and simmer the soup for 15-20 minutes, then puree with a blender.
4. Pour in the cream, stir the soup and serve.

Pea Soup with Coriander

For this pea soup, you will need fresh or frozen green peas.
You'll also need chicken fillets, coriander, and I'll talk about it.
Serve it with sour cream, cream cheese or other toppings to taste.

Ingredients

Green peas – 10 oz
Chicken fillet - 1
Water - 1.5 liters
Coriander - 1 cup
Leek - 1
Olive oil - 1 tablespoon
Spices and seasonings - 1 tablespoon
Garlic - 3 cloves

Instructions

1. Shred the chicken and boil it.
2. Bring the water to the boil, add the peas and simmer for 3 minutes.
3. Chop the leeks and garlic, fry in olive oil and add to the peas.
4. Add the chicken, stir and simmer for 7 minutes.
5. Add the chopped cilantro and spices and puree with a blender.

Zucchini & Herbs Soup Puree

Zucchini puree soup is very simple and very light. So a little herbs will only benefit the dish. Catch a wonderful diet recipe for children and adults for every day!

Ingredients

Zucchini – 18 oz
Cauliflower – 1 cup
Herbs - 1 bundle
Vegetable broth - 2 liters
Spices and seasonings - 1 teaspoon
Salt – to taste

Instructions

1. Chop the vegetables and add to the boiling vegetable broth.
2. Cook for 15-20 minutes on low heat. 5 minutes before the end, add the chopped herbs.
3. Season the soup and puree in a blender.

Asparagus Cream Soup

I really love cream soups. One day I came across this recipe!
Today I want to share it with you - this flavor is completely new
and unlike anything else.

Ingredients

Asparagus – 18 oz
Onion - 1
Butter - 6 tablespoons
Flour - 2 tablespoons
Chicken broth - 2 cups
Cream - 1-2 cups
Spices and seasonings - 1 teaspoon

Instructions

1. Peel the asparagus and chop it finely. Chop the onion.
2. Fry the onion for about 5 minutes in 3 tablespoons of butter.
3. Lightly fry the flour in the remaining butter, pour in the broth and mix.
4. Bring the broth to a boil, add the asparagus and simmer for 20 minutes under a lid over low heat. 5 minutes before the end, add the onion.
5. Puree the soup with a blender, season to taste and add the cream.

Pea Soup Puree

I love making this kind of puree soup in the summer. Garnish it when serving with greens and sprouted grains.

Ingredients

Green peas – 25 oz
Potatoes – 15 oz
Vegetable broth - 1 liter
Onion - 1
Garlic - 1 clove
Herbs – 1 cup
Spices and seasonings - 1 teaspoon

Instructions

1. Finely chop the onion and garlic and fry until transparent.
2. Add the chopped potatoes and continue to fry for 5-7 minutes.
3. Pour boiling broth and boil the soup until the potatoes are cooked.
4. Add the peas and simmer for 5 minutes.
5. Add the spices and herbs and puree the soup in a blender.

Cauliflower Puree Soup with Thyme

If you prefer simple flavors, this cauliflower puree soup is made especially for you. I suggest adding a sprig of aromatic fresh thyme to it.

Ingredients

Cauliflower - 2 cauliflowers
Thyme - 1 sprig
Melted cheese – ½ cup
Vegetable broth - 1 liter
Leek - 1
Garlic - 2 cloves
Olive oil - 2 tablespoons

Instructions

1. Finely chop the onion and garlic and fry in olive oil.
2. Pour in the vegetable broth and bring to the boil.
3. Add the cauliflower florets and cook until soft.
4. Add the melted cheese and stir until it has dissolved.
5. Puree the soup with a blender and add water, broth or milk.
6. Garnish with thyme sprigs when serving.

Rabbit Broth

Rabbit broth can be made if you're on a diet or just cooking for the kids –
I suggest you definitely diversify your diet with this recipe.

Ingredients

Rabbit – 10 oz
Onions - 2
Carrots - 2
Potatoes - 2
Water - 1.5 liters
Dill - 2 tablespoons
Parsley - 2 tablespoons
Salt - 1 teaspoon

Instructions

1. Cover the rabbit with water and boil the broth over a low heat.
2. After 20 minutes, add one carrot and one onion.
3. Boil the broth for 1 hour, and then take out the meat and vegetables. You won't need these vegetables anymore.
4. Send the sliced potatoes into the broth, and after 5-7 minutes, the remaining onion and carrots.
5. Add the rabbit meat and return to the broth, season with salt. Add dill and parsley. Cook until the vegetables are ready.

Salmon Soup with Cream

Do you want to please your family with delicious soup?
With the addition of cream, the soup will have a special taste,
fragrant and delicious.

Ingredients

Salmon – 17 oz
Carrot - 1
Potatoes – 10 oz
Tomatoes - 2
Onions - 1
Garlic - 2 cloves
Cream (20%) - 1 cup
Salt - to taste
Water - 2 liters
Salt – to taste

Instructions

1. Wash the salmon and cut into small pieces.
2. Cut tomatoes, carrots, peeled potatoes and onions.
3. Put the fish, carrots, potatoes in a saucepan with cold water. Boil for 15 minutes after boiling.
4. Add the onions, tomatoes and continue to cook for 10 minutes.
5. Add the cream, salt and cook for 3 minutes on low heat.

Contents

Introduction 3

Chicken & Chickpeas Tomato Soup 4

Rice, Potato & Chicken Kharcho 6

Mashed Potato Soup with Leek 8

Tomato & Bean Soup 10

Salmon, Cod & Pearl Soup 12

Green Borscht with Sorrel 14

Chicken Pea Soup 16

Meat Soup with Beef Tongue 10

Tasty Pea Soup 20

Tomato Mashed Potato Soup with Basil 22

Cauliflower Cream Soup with Broccoli & Feta 24

Pea & Lentil Soup 26

Meat Broth with Noodle 28

Seafood Soup 30

Mashed Potato Soup with Bacon & Cheese 32

Mushroom Soup 34

Pea Soup with Vegetables & Minced Meat 36

Ukrainian Borscht 38

Quail Soup with Halushky 40

Pea Puree Soup with Broccoli 42

Vegetable Soup with Pasta 44

Pork & Chickpeas Soup 46

Chicken Soup with Beans & Spinach 48

Pea Puree Soup with Lentil 50

Pea Soup with Smoked Chicken 52

Vegetarian Kharcho 54

Vegan Pea & Vegetable Soup 56

Sausage & Green Pea Soup 58

Pea & Cabbage Soup 60

Zucchini Cream Soup with Spinach 62

Cheese & Broccoli Soup 64

Asparagus Puree Soup 66

Broccoli & Herbs Soup Puree 68

Tomato Soup with Cream Cheese 70

Chicken Cream Soup 72

Pea Puree Soup with Spinach 74

Celery Puree Soup 76

Spinach & Broccoli Puree Soup 78

Carrot Puree Soup for Children 80

Pea Puree Soup with Mint 82

Zucchini & Cheese Soup Puree 84

Leek Soup 86

Corn Soup Puree 88

Pea Soup with Coriander 90

Zucchini & Herbs Soup Puree 92

Asparagus Cream Soup 94

Pea Soup Puree 96

Cauliflower Puree Soup with Thyme 98

Rabbit Soup 100

Salmon Soup with Cream 102

Contents 104

Made in United States
Troutdale, OR
12/27/2023

16479484R10060